Copyright © 2024 by A Percy and Bumble Creation

All rights reserved.

No portion of this book may be reproduced in any form without written permission from the publisher or author, except as permitted by U.S. copyright law.

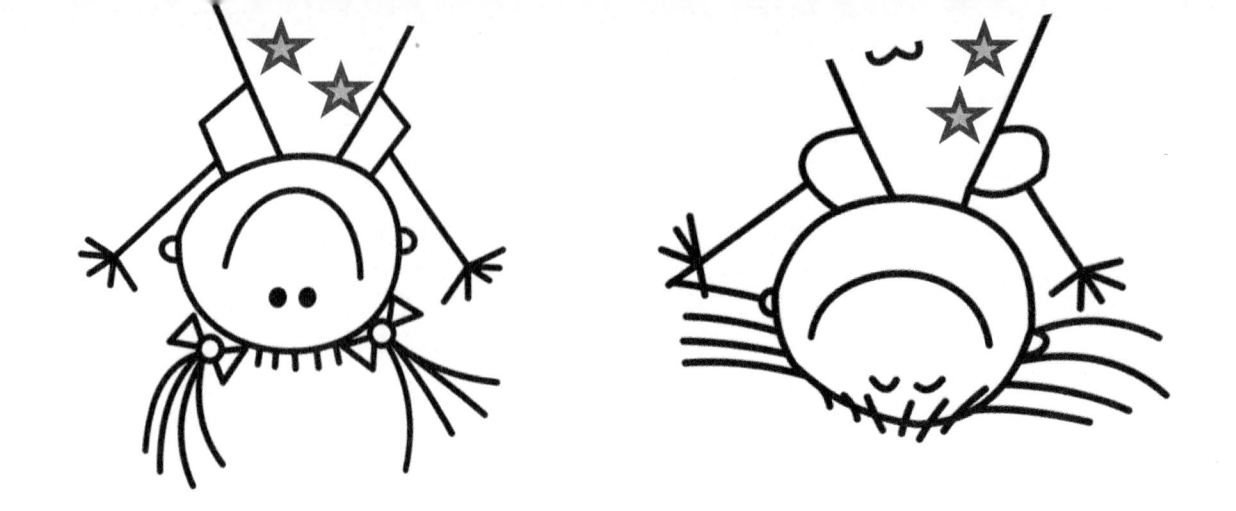

To my two wonderful boys,

Thank you for your boundless enthusiasm, contagious laughter, and endless curiosity, which brought life to every page of this fun-filled farting book. Your creative spark and imaginative spirit has constantly fuelled the hilarity within these pages and has helped keep the characters of Percy and Bumble very much alive. Grandad would be bursting with pride.

May your curious little minds continue to explore and discover the wonders of the world. This book is dedicated to you, my precious little fellas. Enjoy.

This Fabulously Funny Kids Book of Farts belongs to:

....

Contents Page

Contents	Page number
All About this Book	4
Some Science About Farts	6
The Marvel of Digestion	7
Fascinating Farting Funmations that are largely perfectly true	13
Fascinating Farting Funmations that are largely perfectly true even in space	15
What Kind of Fart Are You?	19
Farting Award Scheme	20
Fart Score Sheet Number 1	21
Fart Score Sheet Number 2	27
Fart Score Sheet Number 3	33
Fart Score Sheet Number 4	39
Fart Score Sheet Number 5	45
More Fascinating Farting Funmations that are largely perfectly true, all about animals this time	51
Trouser Trumping Jokes	58

Contents Page

Contents	Page number
Little Poo Maze Puzzle	60
Whizz Stinker Word Search	62
Whiffy Science Word Puzzle	64
Whiffy Science Word Puzzle Clues	66
Windy Word Scramble	68
What Kind of Farter are You – Have You Improved	70
Fart Score Sheet Number 6	71
Fart Score Sheet Number 7	77
Fart Score Sheet Number 8	83
Fart Score Sheet Number 9	89
More Fascinating Farting Funmations that are largely perfectly true	95
Your Last Chance To Achieve the Champion Farter Award	104
Fart Score Sheet Number 10	105
Sketch your Fart	111
Farting Finale Quiz – Test Your New Found Knowledge	114
Answers to Puzzles	118
Final Good Bye	125

All about this book.....

This brilliantly funny and super cool, fun book is all about farts. Yes we said the word didn't we, FARTS!! Let's be honest farts are funny. They smell funny and they certainly sound funny, and everyone does them. Oh yes they do. Do not let anyone pretend otherwise. Everyone does several toots everyday. Your parents do them, your teachers do them, the bus drivers do them, soldiers do them and even our Nannies and Grandpops do them! (Grand "pops" get it?!!)

We just pretend we didn't hear him!

Toot Toot

But as well as being funny, farts are fascinating too and there is loads of science and amazing facts to learn about them. That is what this book is all about. You are going to learn the most surprising and brilliantly cool science behind farts including how they are made, why we do them, who does them the most, and even answers to tremendous questions such as "How fast can a fart travel?" You will even learn about farting in space. You know, just in case you ever go there!

This book is full of farting "Funmations," (our word for "fun" and "information" all rolled up into one fun word!) Fun puzzles, tooting jokes, and more to keep you entertained right to the very end. You can even score your own fart and see if you can win one of the awards inside this book! Yes, it is certificates all around. We really hope you enjoy this fun-filled book and take it in the good-humored spirit that it is designed to be. Now, let the fun and learning begin.....

I can't believe there is actual science behind a bottom burp! Bring it on....

Some Science about Farts

A fart, or flatulence, which is the main scientific name for it, is simply the release of gas that builds up inside of our bodies.

The gas is created when the food we eat starts to get broken down inside of our digestive tract and whilst some people are outraged and disgusted by the sound and smell of a little botty barp, it is actually a very natural process, and everyone does it. Even animals!

But have you ever wondered exactly how a bottom burp is really created? Well, let us find out next because the parping process is far more fascinating than you might think, and there are lots of great and gross things that happen along the way.

I'm going to find out the truth about these Rear End Rippers!

The Marvel of Digestion: A Journey Through Your Body

The Journey begins when we swallow. As soon as this happens the chewed-up food travels down a series of tubes in our body, starting with the esophagus, which connects our throat to our stomach. It uses rhythmic muscle movements, known as peristalsis, to push the food down towards the stomach. Have you ever seen a snake swallow down a large piece of food? Well, peristalsis looks a lot like that!

I bet you didn't think you would be meeting me in a book all about windy whizzers did you!!

Next on this gastronomic journey is the stomach. Think of it as a busy city full of hardworking bacteria, or "good bugs." These diligent little workers are responsible for mixing up all the food we eat and breaking it down into smaller pieces. This is where the process of farting really gets going, but we will come back to that in just a moment.

The little bacteria help churn and mix the food, adding enzymes and acids that help break down hard to digest food into simpler forms that our bodies can use for energy and nutrients to keep us healthy. (Or not if we eat a bad diet!!)

Do you see the good "bacteria" bugs here?

The next stop is the intestines. Once the friendly little bacteria in the stomach have done their job, the partially digested food — now a thick liquid called chyme — gets pushed into our intestines. The intestines are really long hollow tubes located in the lower part of our abdomen. We have two types: a small one and a large one.

The small intestine is where most nutrient absorption happens. Then our food arrives in the large intestine, or colon as it is often called. Its main job is to absorb water and a few other things from the remaining indigestible food matter. Now this is where it starts to get both gross and great all at the same time because the colon also helps in the formation and creation of our poo! Yep, at this stage our body is now telling us that we need to go to the toilet for a good old poop, the proper name for which is faeces. This then brings the journey of food nicely to an end.

So, you see the digestive system is indeed a marvel of nature, working tirelessly to convert the food we eat into energy and nutrients our bodies need and helping us get rid of the bits that we do not need by creating poo! So next time you sit down for a meal, take a moment to appreciate the incredible journey your food is about to embark on.

Now all of this is great and super, but it hasn't told us exactly how a blow-off is created, has it?

So back to the stomach we go. All the hard work by those friendly little bacteria in the stomach and intestines has a side effect which is that gas gets produced when our food is broken down. Once it is produced this gas has to go somewhere, and you guessed it, it comes out of our booty as little, or sometimes even large, toots. So CABOOM, a fart has now been created!!

Hooray for the bacteria!!

But a toot is so much more than just a puff of built-up gas. In fact did you know that each fart is actually made up of lots of different gases? Well, they are, just like this one below…..

- 59% nitrogen,
- 21% hydrogen,
- 9% carbon dioxide,
- 7% methane and
- 4% oxygen

and none of these gasses are even the smelly part! No, the smell comes from the teeny tiny part left over which is less than 1% of the whole toot! Can you believe that? All that smell from just 1% of the entire trouser cough!!

The gas that causes the rear-end ripper to smell is called hydrogen sulfide.

Some foods have lots of sulfide in them and if you eat these you create really stinky farts. You know what this means, don't you?? Of course, it means that if you want to impress, or indeed horrify your friends then make sure you eat loads of food that has got loads of sulfide in it. You will absolutely stink!!

Here is the thing though, if you want to be a "Super Stench Creator" you are going to have to eat a healthy diet, including your greens because some of the foods that contain lots of sulfide include beans, broccoli, cabbage, kale, meat, and eggs.

Watch out teacher, we have all eaten our greens today!!

Fascinating farting funmations that are largely perfectly true!

Funmation 1:

The average person farts between 10 to 20 times per day.

That is 70 to 140 per week, 280 to 560 per month, and 3360 to 6720 per year! WOW INDEED!

I've done my 20 for today!

I've got 3 to go!

Fascinating farting funmations that are largely perfectly true!

Funmation 2:

Did you know that you can measure a fart? Oh yes. There is an instrument called a rectal catheter which is a tube-like thing that can go inside a booty to measure the amount of gas coming out! That does not sound like very much fun for anyone!!!

Fascinating farting funmations that are largely perfectly true, even in space.

Funmation 3:

Ever fancied going to the moon? Do you wonder what might happen if you fart in space, or indeed if it is possible to fart in space?

The answer is YES! It is possible to fart in space. In fact, astronauts regularly fart in space. Before you go getting excited and packing your bags ready for take-off, there are a few more things that you should know about tooting up, up, and beyond.....

Fascinating farting funmations that are largely perfectly true!

Funmation 4

Did you know no one will hear you fart in space! Yes, that's right you can create bottom rippers all you like in space and no one will hear you because for sound waves to travel, air is needed and up in space there is not any air. No air equals no farty sounds!

I thought I heard something there??

Fascinating farting funmations that are largely perfectly true!

Funmation 5.

Farting in space isn't all good news however, and it does have some risks!

Firstly, a space parp could make a small fire slightly worse. This is because some of the gases produced in a fart (hydrogen and methane) become flammable in space. Whilst these gasses are not flammable on Earth, in space they are and when confined in pressurized environments such as space cabins and space centers, this could potentially be a problem!

Get some water quick

Fascinating farting funmations that are largely perfectly true!

Funmation 6

Interestingly it is the smell of a bottom barp that can be more of a problem than the flammable nature. Who would have thought that!!

In space, there is no airflow which means once a stinky little ripper is created it simply lingers for much, much longer. This is why there is a space fart etiquette!! (I'm not sure if there is but there should be by the sounds (and smell) of it!!

Urgh, that will last for ages?

What kind of farter are you?

Now that you know a little bit of the science behind a fart (don't worry there is plenty more to come) have you ever wondered how good you are farting?

Well, here is your chance to find out. Over the next few pages, you can actually score a few of your farts using the criteria provided in this book. How funny is that!! You can even score some more later on to see if you have improved! Find out if you are good enough to achieve the Simple Little Guffer Award or if your windy efforts are worthy of a much higher accolade. Best of luck to you.

Farting Award Scheme

Score out of 10	Farting Award
1 out of 10	The Simple Little Guffer Award
2 out of 10	The Rinker Stinker Tinker Award
3 out of 10	The Great and Glorious Gas Guffer Award
4 out of 10	The Deadliest Gut Dropper Award
5 out of 10	The Truly Terrific Tooter Award
6 out of 10	The Frighteningly Ferocious Farter Award
7 out of 10	The Brilliant Barping Bottom Burper Award
8 out of 10	The Outstandingly Offensive Aroma Award
9 out of 10	The Supremely Superb Stench Creater Award
10 out of 10	Chief Champion and Farter Extraordinaire Award

Fart Score Sheet number 1

Date: ....

Time of Day: ....

Location: ....

Expected/Unexpected/Delayed

Position during Fart: (Circle the answer)

Standing / Sitting / Lying / Kneeling / Moving

Grade your fart stench using the following criteria:
- ☐ Mildy stinky
- ☐ Offensive
- ☐ So bad you could taste it
- ☐ So strong you had to leave the room
- ☐ It made you actually vomit

Based on the above rating give your Fart a name:
_____

Yuk!

(Enter your fart's name here)............................was created in:

Public/Private/A Crowded area (circle as appropriate)

Following the immediate creation of (enter your fart's name here)................................ I felt extremely:

Embarrassed/Proud/Triumphant/Scared/Worried about yourself (circle as appropriate)

Did your fart cause others to:

Scream	Yes/No
Run	Yes/No
Grimace	Yes/No
Vomit	Yes/No
Laugh	Yes/No

Following your fart did you:

Confess	Yes/No
Blame someone else	Yes/No
Deny it	Yes/No
Pretend it didn't Happen	Yes/No
Celebrate	Yes/No

Grade the Volume of your Fart against the following criteria

☐ It definitely made your underpants cough

☐ You had to shout just to be heard over the sound of your fart

☐ You felt the floor beneath you shake and a few things fell off the shelf

☐ The Dog ran under the sofa thinking it was a jet plane coming into land

☐ There was an immediate news flash with the Prime Minister announcing the country was under attack

Cough cough, what was that??

Ooo

Reflections and Key learnings:

What were the 3 best things about your fart:

1:

2:

3:

What were the 3 worst things about your fart:

1:

2:

3:

What are 3 things you can do differently next time:

1:

2:

3:

Take a moment to look back and review how you have evaluated your fart so far and then give your fantastic little toot an overall score out of 10.

……../10

Turn to page 20 to check the Farting Award Scheme and see what level you have achieved. Then you can complete your very own cut-out and keep bottom barping certificate. Hoorah!

Congratulations

You have achieved the

....

....

Your efforts are truly outstanding. Keep up the amazing work

Fart Score Sheet number 2

Date: ....

Time of Day: ....

Location: ....

Expected/Unexpected/Delayed

Position during Fart: (Circle the answer)

Standing / Sitting / Lying / Kneeling / Moving

Grade your fart stench using the following criteria:
- ❑ Mildy stinky
- ❑ Offensive
- ❑ So bad you could taste it
- ❑ So strong you had to leave the room
- ❑ It made you actually vomit

Based on the above rating give your Fart a name:
_____

YUK!

(Enter your fart's name here)……………………………was created in:

Public/Private/A Crowded area (circle as appropriate)

Following the immediate creation of (enter your fart's name here)…………………………… I felt extremely:

Embarrassed/Proud/Triumphant/Scared/Worried about yourself (circle as appropriate)

Did your fart cause others to:

Scream	Yes/No
Run	Yes/No
Grimace	Yes/No
Vomit	Yes/No
Laugh	Yes/No

Following your fart did you:

Confess	Yes/No
Blame someone else	Yes/No
Deny it	Yes/No
Pretend it didn't Happen	Yes/No
Celebrate	Yes/No

Grade the Volume of your Fart against the following criteria

☐ It definitely made your underpants cough

☐ You had to shout just to be heard over the sound of your fart

☐ You felt the floor beneath you shake and a few things fell off the shelf

☐ The Dog ran under the sofa thinking it was a jet plane coming into land

☐ There was an immediate news flash with the Prime Minister announcing the country was under attack

Reflections and Key learnings:

What were the 3 best things about your fart:

1:

2:

3:

What were the 3 worst things about your fart:

1:

2:

3:

What are 3 things you can do differently next time:

1:

2:

3:

Take a moment to look back and review how you have evaluated your fart so far and then give your fantastic little toot an overall score out of 10.

……../10

Turn to page 20 to check the Farting Award Scheme and see what level you have achieved. Then you can complete your very own cut out and keep bottom barping certificate. Hoorah!

Congratulations

You have achieved the

....

....

Your efforts are truly outstanding. Keep up the amazing work

Fart score Sheet number 3

Date: ....

Time of Day: ....

Location: ....

Expected/Unexpected/Delayed

Position during Fart: (Circle the answer)

Standing / Sitting / Lying / Kneeling / Moving

Grade your fart stench using the following criteria:

- ☐ Mildy stinky
- ☐ Offensive
- ☐ So bad you could taste it
- ☐ So strong you had to leave the room
- ☐ It made you actually vomit

Based on the above rating give your Fart a name:

_____

(Enter your fart's name here)..................................was created in:

Public/Private/A Crowded area (circle as appropriate)

Following the immediate creation of (enter your fart's name here)................................. I felt extremely:

Embarrassed/Proud/Triumphant/Scared/Worried about yourself (circle as appropriate)

Did your fart cause others to:

Scream	Yes/No
Run	Yes/No
Grimace	Yes/No
Vomit	Yes/No
Laugh	Yes/No

Following your fart did you:

Confess	Yes/No
Blame someone else	Yes/No
Deny it	Yes/No
Pretend it didn't Happen	Yes/No
Celebrate	Yes/No

Grade the Volume of your Fart against the following criteria

☐ It definitely made your underpants cough

☐ You had to shout just to be heard over the sound of your fart

☐ You felt the floor beneath you shake and a few things fell off the shelf

☐ The Dog ran under the sofa thinking it was a jet plane coming into land

☐ There was an immediate news flash with the Prime Minister announcing the country was under attack

Reflections and Key learnings:

What were the 3 best things about your fart:

1:

2:

3:

What were the 3 worst things about your fart:

1:

2:

3:

What are 3 things you can do differently next time:

1:

2:

3:

Take a moment to look back and review how you have evaluated your fart so far and then give your fantastic little toot an overall score out of 10.

……../10

Turn to page 20 to check the Farting Award Scheme and see what level you have achieved. Then you can complete your very own cut out and keep bottom barping certificate. Hoorah!

Congratulations

You have achieved the

....

....

Your efforts are truly outstanding. Keep up the amazing work

Fart Score Sheet number 4

Date: ....

Time of Day: ....

Location: ....

Expected/Unexpected/Delayed

Position during Fart: (Circle the answer)

Standing / Sitting / Lying / Kneeling / Moving

Grade your fart stench using the following criteria:

- ☐ Mildy stinky
- ☐ Offensive
- ☐ So bad you could taste it
- ☐ So strong you had to leave the room
- ☐ It made you actually vomit

Based on the above rating give your Fart a name:

YUK!

(Enter your fart's name here)............................was created in:

Public/Private/A Crowded area (circle as appropriate)

Following the immediate creation of (enter your fart's name here)............................. I felt extremely:

Embarrassed/Proud/Triumphant/Scared/Worried about yourself (circle as appropriate)

Did your fart cause others to:

Scream	Yes/No
Run	Yes/No
Grimace	Yes/No
Vomit	Yes/No
Laugh	Yes/No

Following your fart did you:

Confess	Yes/No
Blame someone else	Yes/No
Deny it	Yes/No
Pretend it didn't Happen	Yes/No
Celebrate	Yes/No

Grade the Volume of your Fart against the following criteria

☐ It definitely made your underpants cough

☐ You had to shout just to be heard over the sound of your fart

☐ You felt the floor beneath you shake and a few things fell off the shelf

☐ The Dog ran under the sofa thinking it was a jet plane coming into land

☐ There was an immediate news flash with the Prime Minister announcing the country was under attack

Reflections and Key learnings:

What were the 3 best things about your fart:

1:

2:

3:

What were the 3 worst things about your fart:

1:

2:

3:

What are 3 things you can do differently next time:

1:

2:

3:

Take a moment to look back and review how you have evaluated your fart so far and then give your fantastic little toot an overall score out of 10.

……../10

Turn to page 20 to check the Farting Award Scheme and see what level you have achieved. Then you can complete your very own cut out and keep bottom barping certificate. Hoorah!

Congratulations

You have achieved the

....

....

Your efforts are truly outstanding. Keep up the amazing work

Fart Score Sheet number 5

Date: ....

Time of Day: ....

Location: ....

Expected/Unexpected/Delayed

Position during Fart: (Circle the answer)

Standing / Sitting / Lying / Kneeling / Moving

Grade your fart stench using the following criteria:

- ☐ Mildy stinky
- ☐ Offensive
- ☐ So bad you could taste it
- ☐ So strong you had to leave the room
- ☐ It made you actually vomit

Based on the above rating give your Fart a name:
_____

(Enter your fart's name here)..was created in:

Public/Private/A Crowded area (circle as appropriate)

Following the immediate creation of (enter your fart's name here).................................... I felt extremely:

Embarrassed/Proud/Triumphant/Scared/Worried about yourself (circle as appropriate)

Did your fart cause others to:

Scream	Yes/No
Run	Yes/No
Grimace	Yes/No
Vomit	Yes/No
Laugh	Yes/No

Following your fart did you:

Confess	Yes/No
Blame someone else	Yes/No
Deny it	Yes/No
Pretend it didn't Happen	Yes/No
Celebrate	Yes/No

Grade the Volume of your Fart against the following criteria

- ❏ It definitely made your underpants cough

- ❏ You had to shout just to be heard over the sound of your fart

- ❏ You felt the floor beneath you shake and a few things fell off the shelf

- ❏ The Dog ran under the sofa thinking it was a jet plane coming into land

- ❏ There was an immediate news flash with the Prime Minister announcing the country was under attack

Reflections and Key learnings:

What were the 3 best things about your fart:

1:

2:

3:

What were the 3 worst things about your fart:

1:

2:

3:

What are 3 things you can do differently next time:

1:

2:

3:

Take a moment to look back and review how you have evaluated your fart so far and then give your fantastic little toot an overall score out of 10.

………/10

Turn to page 20 to check the Farting Award Scheme and see what level you have achieved. Then you can complete your very own cut out and keep bottom barping certificate. Hoorah!

Congratulations

You have achieved the

....

....

Your efforts are truly outstanding. Keep up the amazing work

More fascinating farting funmations that are largely perfectly true! All about animals this time.

Funmation 7:

It is not just humans that fart you know. Animals can be pretty stinky too. In fact, cows are notorious for their methane-producing farts which contribute significantly to greenhouse gas emissions, if you can believe that! Next time you visit a farm don't get too close to the cows!

Fascinating farting funmations that are largely perfectly true!

Funmation 8:

Now this is a good one. Termites, remember, those little tiny guys? Well, they are also one of the biggest culprits of methane production through farting. Despite their tiny little size, they produce more methane than even cows! INCREDIBLE! It's mainly due to their huge population size all over the world. Now that is surprising, isn't it?

I am a champion methane producer!!

Fascinating farting funmations that are largely perfectly true!

Funmation 9:

This one is brilliant...Some animals use farts as a form of communication, for example, the Atlantic Herring releases bubbles from its back end as part of a nocturnal communication system - this is called an "FRT" or Fast Repetitive Tick. Although this is not technically a bottom burp, it basically means they have their own farting code! That is just soooo cool!

Well how kind of you to say so!

Fascinating farting funmations that are largely perfectly true!

Funmation 10:

Now let's talk about the whale. This whopper of a mammal produces a whopper of a fart! Yes, they definitely do release gas! They do it in a similar way to us because their digestive system is similar to ours. Rather impressively whale flatulence can be hugely potent because of the large number of stinky fish they eat. That however is not the end of it….. After a whale dies this gas can continue to build up inside its body until it actually explodes! Yes, that's right, an exploding, gas-filled farting whale is an actual thing!!! WHO KNEW THAT THEN?

Fascinating farting funmations that are largely perfectly true!

Funmation 11:

Interestingly, not all animals pass wind. Take birds for example, they do not fart. This is because their gastrointestinal system doesn't produce the same gaseous byproducts that mammals do during digestion. Instead, they expel waste in one go through their cloaca. (their version of our bottom!)

No one will hear my bottom burp!!

Fascinating farting funmations that are largely perfectly true!

Funmation 12:

Now, even though they are small, insects do pass gas too, the process however is quite different from how we do it. You see Insects have a system called the tracheal system that allows them to exchange gases directly with their environment. This means they breathe in oxygen and breathe out carbon dioxide through tiny tubes called spiracles located on their bodies. I suppose then that technically we cannot say that insects actually fart. That's a shame, it would be great to hear a spider fart, wouldn't it!!

Fascinating farting funmations that are largely perfectly true!

Funmation 13:

Cockroaches (Yuk) produce methane gas as part of their digestive process just like us. However, cockroaches only release this gas when they die. This means that while a living cockroach might not technically fart, a dead one actually creates a deathly smell!

Why me? Dead cockroaches stink

Trouser Trumping Jokes

1: Why did the teacher stop telling fart jokes?

2: Farting on an elevator is very bad.

3: Why do you have to be careful of ninjas' farts?

4: Why did the fart miss school?

5: What do you call a dinosaur fart?

6: What does everyone know about a clown's fart?

7: Why won't the skeleton enter a tooting contest??

8: Why did the fart go to school?

9: Why could a fart never be a secret agent?

10: What is a fart's favorite planet?

Trouser Trumping Answers

1: She was told that her jokes stink.

2: It is just wrong on so many levels.

3: Because they are silent but deadly.

4: It got expelled.

5: A blast from the past.

6: It always smells funny.

7: It doesn't have the guts.

8: To get some "toot" oring.

9: They always leave a trail behind.

10: Uranus.

Little Poo Maze Puzzle

Can you help little poo find his way to the toilet through the maze? Look at the back of this book for the answer

Start here

This is a simple bleed through page so that your pens do not mark the next page. It protects the ever so funny pages after each puzzle.

The Wizz Stinker Word Search

See if you can find all 12 words below that are associated with the science of bottom burps. Find the answers at the back of this book.

```
J H L V U I P C I B D W Z Z J V D Z S F R
U I U Q U X S J F F K J C D H B K I Q I O
M X R G O I V H O N C S T P H V N S E B B
I T D M A S K D O F P F Z U D H O Q C M F
T P R L O S S I D L O Q S L R U W F O W P
Z L M O H F T Q P D D C M Y T S M U L I B
W I M R N S G R P T O M W K T O R N O U I
Y T E K E X U A O R R X N Y H U T M N T C
L M W G Y B I G L I M M M W P J F L F H E
R B I X Z R L H C B N Y I Z W Z L P M V K
V D A O E Q H V C W F T T U Q Z A H T E K
F G T T T N A E J C N F E I A L T M W U B
M C C L S H G M R J R G I S U Y U S D B D
H A N L I N T E S T I N E S T W L T U H Z
B M A R B Q G K K N Z M G G U I E O X Z L
P M E T H A N E J E S U K O H U N M O S N
E X N F U F O C I A B D G M X M C A T G Y
I H I X F P M A P O Q R Z T Y U E C L R N
T C S O A G J X M U I X D I W C P H J K M
N N V F T E P Z M B O L R D A M N K T Y R
G N M G B T C N Y I D Z C P G A S Q F P V
```

GAS   ODOR   BURP
FOOD   COLON   METHANE
STOMACH   BACTERIA   DIGESTION
FLATULENCE   INTESTINES   GASTROINTESTINAL

This is a simple bleed through page so that your pens do not mark the next page. It protects the ever-so-funny pages after each puzzle.

The Whiffy Science Word Puzzle

Use the clues on the next page to see if you can complete the word puzzle. Remember this is all about the science behind tooting. Good luck. Find the answers at the back of this book.

This is a simple bleed through page so that your pens do not mark the next page. It protects the ever so funny pages after each puzzle.

The Whiffy Science Word Puzzle Clues

Across:

1 - It is the process used by your body to turn food into energy and sometimes gas.

5 - This is where gas builds up before it is released from your body.

7 - A tight muscle that helps control when the wind comes out of your body.

10 - Another scientific word for Toot.

11 - A gas that forms part of the gas produced in a fart.

12 - This is the food that we eat and it can affect how smelly the bottom whizzers are.

The Whiffy Science Word Puzzle Clues

Down:

2 - The scientific name for the gas that comes out of your bottom.

3 - The tiny living things in your gut that breakdown food and cause gas.

4 - A gas that is often found in a fart and is also part of natural gas.

6 - Little organisms that live in your gut and produce gas as they work.

8 - The squeezing motion used by your gut to move food along.

9 - The final part of your digestive tract where gas waits before being released.

Windy Word Scramble

Can you rearrange the letters to reveal 20 words, all associated with rear-end rippers? The first one has been done for you as an example. Find the answers at the end of the book.

sGa	= Gas	eMnetha	= _____
intsgiDeo	= _____	etsnInesit	= _____
aeaBticr	= _____	olnCo	= _____
lautsF	= _____	Odro	= _____
telonniratsiGats	= _____	oelBw	= _____
emuRct	= _____	saesG	= _____
ntraiFemenot	= _____	ocMsrebi	= _____
tGu	= _____	iulgmbnR	= _____
onrctexEi	= _____	uoFl	= _____
rgyHenod	= _____	uSlurf	= _____

This is a simple bleed through page so that your pens do not mark the next page. It protects the ever so funny pages after each puzzle.

What kind of farter are you? Have you improved?

So, you are clever enough to have completed the puzzles, but are your little rump ripplers improving as your farting knowledge expands? Can you gain a higher award? Find out by scoring some more of your farts next.

I think I might have a go this time. Hee hee.

Fart score Sheet number 6

Date: ....

Time of Day: ....

Location: ....

Expected/Unexpected/Delayed

Position during Fart: (Circle the answer)

Standing / Sitting / Lying / Kneeling / Moving

Grade your fart stench using the following criteria:
- ☐ Mildy stinky
- ☐ Offensive
- ☐ So bad you could taste it
- ☐ So strong you had to leave the room
- ☐ It made you actually vomit

Based on the above rating give your Fart a name:
_____

(Enter your fart's name here)..................................was created in:

Public/Private/A Crowded area (circle as appropriate)

Following the immediate creation of (enter your fart's name here)................................... I felt extremely:

Embarrassed/Proud/Triumphant/Scared/Worried about yourself (circle as appropriate)

Did your fart cause others to:

Scream	Yes/No
Run	Yes/No
Grimace	Yes/No
Vomit	Yes/No
Laugh	Yes/No

Following your fart did you:

Confess	Yes/No
Blame someone else	Yes/No
Deny it	Yes/No
Pretend it didn't Happen	Yes/No
Celebrate	Yes/No

Grade the Volume of your Fart against the following criteria

☐ It definitely made your underpants cough

☐ You had to shout just to be heard over the sound of your fart

☐ You felt the floor beneath you shake and a few things fell off the shelf

☐ The Dog ran under the sofa thinking it was a jet plane coming into land

☐ There was an immediate news flash with the Prime Minister announcing the country was under attack

Reflections and Key learnings:

What were the 3 best things about your fart:

1:

2:

3:

What were the 3 worst things about your fart:

1:

2:

3:

What are 3 things you can do differently next time:

1:

2:

3:

Take a moment to look back and review how you have evaluated your fart so far and then give your fantastic little toot an overall score out of 10.

………/10

Turn to page 20 to check the Farting Award Scheme and see what level you have achieved. Then you can complete your very own cut out and keep bottom barping certificate. Hoorah!

Congratulations

You have achieved the

....

....

Your efforts are truly outstanding. Keep up the amazing work

Fart score Sheet number 7

Date: ....

Time of Day: ....

Location: ....

Expected/Unexpected/Delayed

Position during Fart: (Circle the answer)

Standing / Sitting / Lying / Kneeling / Moving

Grade your fart stench using the following criteria:

- ☐ Mildy stinky
- ☐ Offensive
- ☐ So bad you could taste it
- ☐ So strong you had to leave the room
- ☐ It made you actually vomit

Based on the above rating give your Fart a name:

_____

(Enter your fart's name here)............................was created in:

Public/Private/A Crowded area (circle as appropriate)

Following the immediate creation of (enter your fart's name here)............................ I felt extremely:

Embarrassed/Proud/Triumphant/Scared/Worried about yourself (circle as appropriate)

Did your fart cause others to:

Scream	Yes/No
Run	Yes/No
Grimace	Yes/No
Vomit	Yes/No
Laugh	Yes/No

Following your fart did you:

Confess	Yes/No
Blame someone else	Yes/No
Deny it	Yes/No
Pretend it didn't Happen	Yes/No
Celebrate	Yes/No

Grade the Volume of your Fart against the following criteria

☐ It definitely made your underpants cough

☐ You had to shout just to be heard over the sound of your fart

☐ You felt the floor beneath you shake and a few things fell off the shelf

☐ The Dog ran under the sofa thinking it was a jet plane coming into land

☐ There was an immediate news flash with the Prime Minister announcing the country was under attack

Reflections and Key learnings:

What were the 3 best things about your fart:

1:

2:

3:

What were the 3 worst things about your fart:

1:

2:

3:

What are 3 things you can do differently next time:

1:

2:

3:

Take a moment to look back and review how you have evaluated your fart so far and then give your fantastic little toot an overall score out of 10.

……../10

Turn to page 20 to check the Farting Award Scheme and see what level you have achieved. Then you can complete your very own cut out and keep bottom barping certificate. Hoorah!

Congratulations

You have achieved the

....

....

Your efforts are truly outstanding. Keep up the amazing work

Fart Score Sheet number 8

Date: ....

Time of Day: ....

Location: ....

Expected/Unexpected/Delayed

Position during Fart: (Circle the answer)

Standing / Sitting / Lying / Kneeling / Moving

Grade your fart stench using the following criteria:

- ☐ Mildy stinky
- ☐ Offensive
- ☐ So bad you could taste it
- ☐ So strong you had to leave the room
- ☐ It made you actually vomit

Based on the above rating give your Fart a name:
_____

(Enter your fart's name here)..................................was created in:

Public/Private/A Crowded area (circle as appropriate)

Following the immediate creation of (enter your fart's name here)............................... I felt extremely:

Embarrassed/Proud/Triumphant/Scared/Worried about yourself (circle as appropriate)

Did your fart cause others to:

Scream	Yes/No
Run	Yes/No
Grimace	Yes/No
Vomit	Yes/No
Laugh	Yes/No

Following your fart did you:

Confess	Yes/No
Blame someone else	Yes/No
Deny it	Yes/No
Pretend it didn't Happen	Yes/No
Celebrate	Yes/No

Grade the Volume of your Fart against the following criteria

☐ It definitely made your underpants cough

☐ You had to shout just to be heard over the sound of your fart

☐ You felt the floor beneath you shake and a few things fell off the shelf

☐ The Dog ran under the sofa thinking it was a jet plane coming into land

☐ There was an immediate news flash with the Prime Minister announcing the country was under attack

Reflections and Key learnings:

What were the 3 best things about your fart:

1:

2:

3:

What were the 3 worst things about your fart:

1:

2:

3:

What are 3 things you can do differently next time:

1:

2:

3:

Take a moment to look back and review how you have evaluated your fart so far and then give your fantastic little toot an overall score out of 10.

………/10

Turn to page 20 to check the Farting Award Scheme and see what level you have achieved. Then you can complete your very own cut out and keep bottom barping certificate. Hoorah!

Congratulations

You have achieved the

....

....

Your efforts are truly outstanding. Keep up the amazing work

Fart Score Sheet number 9

Date: ....

Time of Day: ....

Location: ....

Expected/Unexpected/Delayed

Position during Fart: (Circle the answer)

Standing / Sitting / Lying / Kneeling / Moving

Grade your fart stench using the following criteria:

- ❏ Mildy stinky
- ❏ Offensive
- ❏ So bad you could taste it
- ❏ So strong you had to leave the room
- ❏ It made you actually vomit

Based on the above rating give your Fart a name:

_____

YUK!

(Enter your fart's name here)............................was created in:

Public/Private/A Crowded area (circle as appropriate)

Following the immediate creation of (enter your fart's name here)............................... I felt extremely:

Embarrassed/Proud/Triumphant/Scared/Worried about yourself (circle as appropriate)

Did your fart cause others to:

Scream   Yes/No
Run   Yes/No
Grimace   Yes/No
Vomit   Yes/No
Laugh   Yes/No

Following your fart did you:

Confess   Yes/No
Blame someone else   Yes/No
Deny it   Yes/No
Pretend it didn't Happen
                       Yes/No
Celebrate   Yes/No

Grade the Volume of your Fart against the following criteria

☐ It definitely made your underpants cough

☐ You had to shout just to be heard over the sound of your fart

☐ You felt the floor beneath you shake and a few things fell off the shelf

☐ The Dog ran under the sofa thinking it was a jet plane coming into land

☐ There was an immediate news flash with the Prime Minister announcing the country was under attack

Reflections and Key learnings:

What were the 3 best things about your fart:

1:

2:

3:

What were the 3 worst things about your fart:

1:

2:

3:

What are 3 things you can do differently next time:

1:

2:

3:

Take a moment to look back and review how you have evaluated your fart so far and then give your fantastic little toot an overall score out of 10.

………/10

Turn to page 20 to check the Farting Award Scheme and see what level you have achieved. Then you can complete your very own cut out and keep bottom barping certificate. Hoorah!

Congratulations

You have achieved the

....

....

Your efforts are truly outstanding. Keep up the amazing work

Fascinating farting funmations that are largely perfectly true!

Funmation 14:

So, if you find jokes about farts funny, don't be embarrassed, you are not alone. Did you know for example that the oldest recorded joke is actually about a fart? Yes indeed!

The joke goes all the way back to 1900BC and is about a lady who may or may not have tooted in her husband's lap. Who would have thought the olden days would be so funny!!

Fascinating farting funmations that are largely perfectly true!

Funmation 15:

Remarkably there are actually places where excessive tooting is considered illegal! Gosh, that's strict! In Malawi, Africa, legislation was passed in 2011 making public bottom burping illegal under the "Air Fouling Legislation". Imagine if you accidentally ate too many baked beans for lunch!!

WANTED

Any person who lets rip too often shall be severely punished

Fascinating farting funmations that are largely perfectly true!

Funmation 16:

Have you ever wondered how much actual space a bottom burp takes up? Well, it turns out that a group of scientists wondered the same thing back in 1991. They discovered that the volume of an average fart was between 33 and 125 mls. Compare this to the volume of a can of fizzy drink, which is 330mls, and the answer is that farts really don't take up too much room at all unless of course, you do lots and lots and lots and lots and lots of them all in one go!!!

Do you have room for just one more?

Fascinating farting funmations that are largely perfectly true!

Funmation 17:

Imagine if you could earn money through farting! Well, rather unbelievably you can! Yes, as incredible as it sounds there are actually professional fart smellers! Urgh, can you imagine having to do that all day long? Even though it sounds most disgusting it is actually really useful because a professional stench smeller can detect certain smells within a toot which can then help determine the presence of disease!! Personally, I think some things are best left to other types of smellers....

Ahh yes I am definitely on to something here...

Fascinating farting funmations that are largely perfectly true!

Funmation 18:

Did you know that on average we bottom burp enough gas each day to fill up an entire balloon? Bring on those birthday parties!!

Oh if only they knew how I filled this balloon up!!

Fascinating farting funmations that are largely perfectly true!

Funmation 19:

Have you ever wondered how fast a fart can travel? Well, wonder no more because a fart can be expelled out of the rear at a speed of almost 7 miles per hour! That's faster than I can run!!!

Help me, my ripper is catching me up!

Fascinating farting funmations that are largely perfectly true!

Funmation 20:

Did you know that the ancient Japanese were said to have held "farting contests" to see who could break wind the loudest and longest? What brilliantly stinky contests they must have been

Funmation 21:

Here is something to think about the next time you go on an airplane. Did you know that it is much easier to create bottom whizzers on an airplane than on land? This is all due to the cabin pressure which causes more intestinal gas to build up. The awful thing is that cabin air is largely recycled. Yuk indeed.

Fascinating farting funmations that are largely perfectly true!

Funmation 22:

The world record for the longest continuous fart is held by a man named Bernard Clemmens from London. He managed to sustain a flatulent wind for an astounding 2 minutes and 42 seconds. This impressive feat was achieved in 1979, and it still stands unbroken today.

Incredible indeed!

Fascinating farting funmations that are largely perfectly true!

Funmation 23:

Have you ever wanted to run up to someone and just let off a bottom biscuit? Well, there is a tribe of people who live in the Amazon who do just that! The Yanomami Tribe literally greet each other with a jolly good fart. What a wonderful way to say hello to your bestie!!

Toot Toot

And hello to you too bestie

This is your last chance to Achieve the champion farter Award.

With so few pages left, this is your last chance to use everything that have learned and laughed about so far. One final push (get it?) to see what kind of farter you really are...

Fart score Sheet number 10

Date: ....

Time of Day: ....

Location: ....

Expected/Unexpected/Delayed

Position during Fart: (Circle the answer)

Standing / Sitting / Lying / Kneeling / Moving

Grade your fart stench using the following criteria:

- ☐ Mildy stinky
- ☐ Offensive
- ☐ So bad you could taste it
- ☐ So strong you had to leave the room
- ☐ It made you actually vomit

Based on the above rating give your Fart a name:

(Enter your fart's name here)..................................was created in:

Public/Private/A Crowded area (circle as appropriate)

Following the immediate creation of (enter your fart's name here)............................. I felt extremely:

Embarrassed/Proud/Triumphant/Scared/Worried about yourself (circle as appropriate)

Did your fart cause others to:

Scream	Yes/No
Run	Yes/No
Grimace	Yes/No
Vomit	Yes/No
Laugh	Yes/No

Following your fart did you:

Confess	Yes/No
Blame someone else	Yes/No
Deny it	Yes/No
Pretend it didn't Happen	Yes/No
Celebrate	Yes/No

Grade the Volume of your Fart against the following criteria

- ❏ It definitely made your underpants cough

- ❏ You had to shout just to be heard over the sound of your fart

- ❏ You felt the floor beneath you shake and a few things fell off the shelf

- ❏ The Dog ran under the sofa thinking it was a jet plane coming into land

- ❏ There was an immediate news flash with the Prime Minister announcing the country was under attack

Cough cough, what was that??

Reflections and Key learnings:

What were the 3 best things about your fart:

1:

2:

3:

What were the 3 worst things about your fart:

1:

2:

3:

What are 3 things you can do differently next time:

1:

2:

3:

Take a moment to look back and review how you have evaluated your fart so far and then give your fantastic little toot an overall score out of 10.

………/10

Turn to page 20 to check the Farting Award Scheme and see what level you have achieved. Then you can complete your very own cut out and keep bottom barping certificate. Hoorah!

Congratulations

You have achieved the

....

....

Your efforts are truly outstanding. Keep up the amazing work

Feel free to draw or sketch your champion bottom belcher here. You know you deserve it.

This is a simple bleed through page so that your pens do not mark the next page. It protects the ever so funny pages after your super sketch.

What a fantastic achievement, you have now collected lots of Farting Award Certificates, very well done indeed. Keep them safe and show them to your friends.

Now let's see how much you know about farts as you turn the page to complete the farting finale quiz....

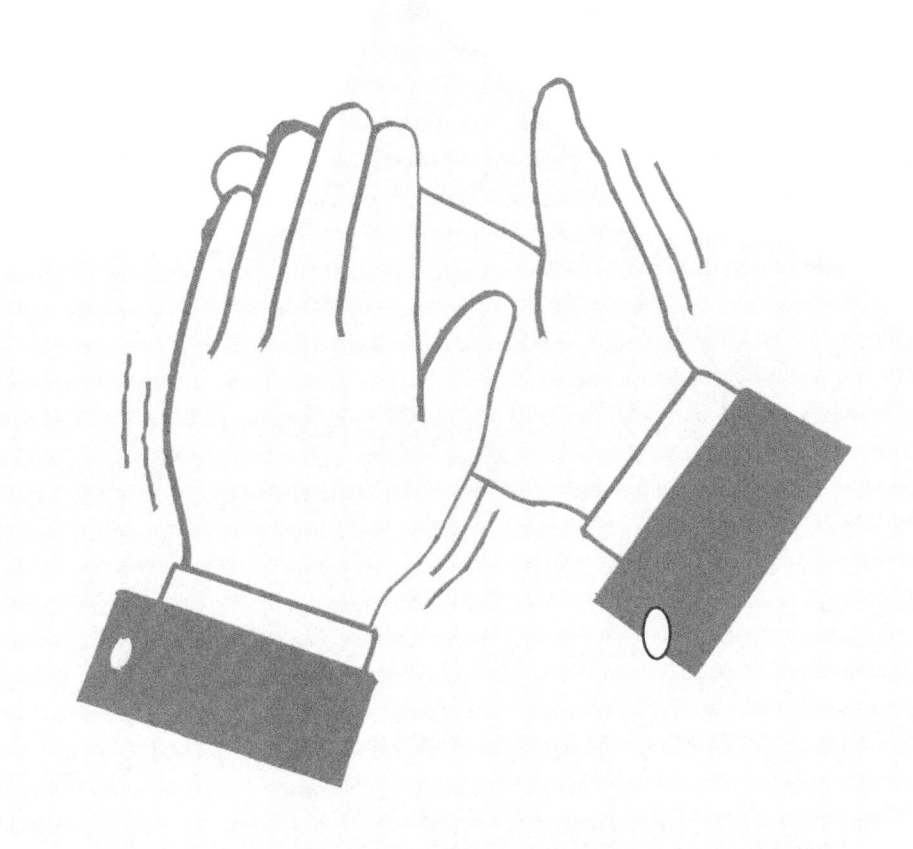

The Farting Finale Quiz.

Let's see how much incredible and totally awesome gas-guffing knowledge you have gained with this farting finale quiz. Simply answer as many questions as you can.

Part 1

1. Fill in the blank: The average person farts _____ times a day.

2. True or False: All animals fart.

3. Fill in the blank: The gas that gives farts their notorious smell is called _____.

4. Which animal's fart has been known to cause explosions because of its high methane content?
_____

5. Fill in the blank: Farting, also known as _____, is a natural process of digestion.

The farting finale Quiz
Part 2

1. What is the primary gas component of a fart?

    A. Oxygen

    B. Nitrogen

    C. Carbon Dioxide

    D. Methane

2. Which animal is known to produce the most methane through farting?

    A. Dogs

    B. Cows

    C. Elephants

    D. Horses

The farting finale Quiz
Part 2

3. Why do farts sometimes smell bad?

   A. Because of undigested food particles.

   B. Due to sulfur-containing gases.

   C. They actually don't smell, it's just our imagination.

   D. It's because of the oxygen content.

4. What causes the sound of a fart?

   A. The amount of gas produced.

   B. The speed at which it is expelled.

   C. The vibration of the rectal opening.

   D. All of the above.

The farting finale Quiz
Part 2

5. Can holding in farts be harmful?

   A. Yes, it can cause discomfort and bloating.

   B. No, it has no effect on health whatsoever.

   C. It can lead to spontaneous human combustion.

   D. It can cause memory loss.

6. What purpose does farting serve for some fish species?

   A. Communication

   B. Digestion

   C. Buoyancy control

   D. Attracting mates

Little Poo Maze Puzzle Answer

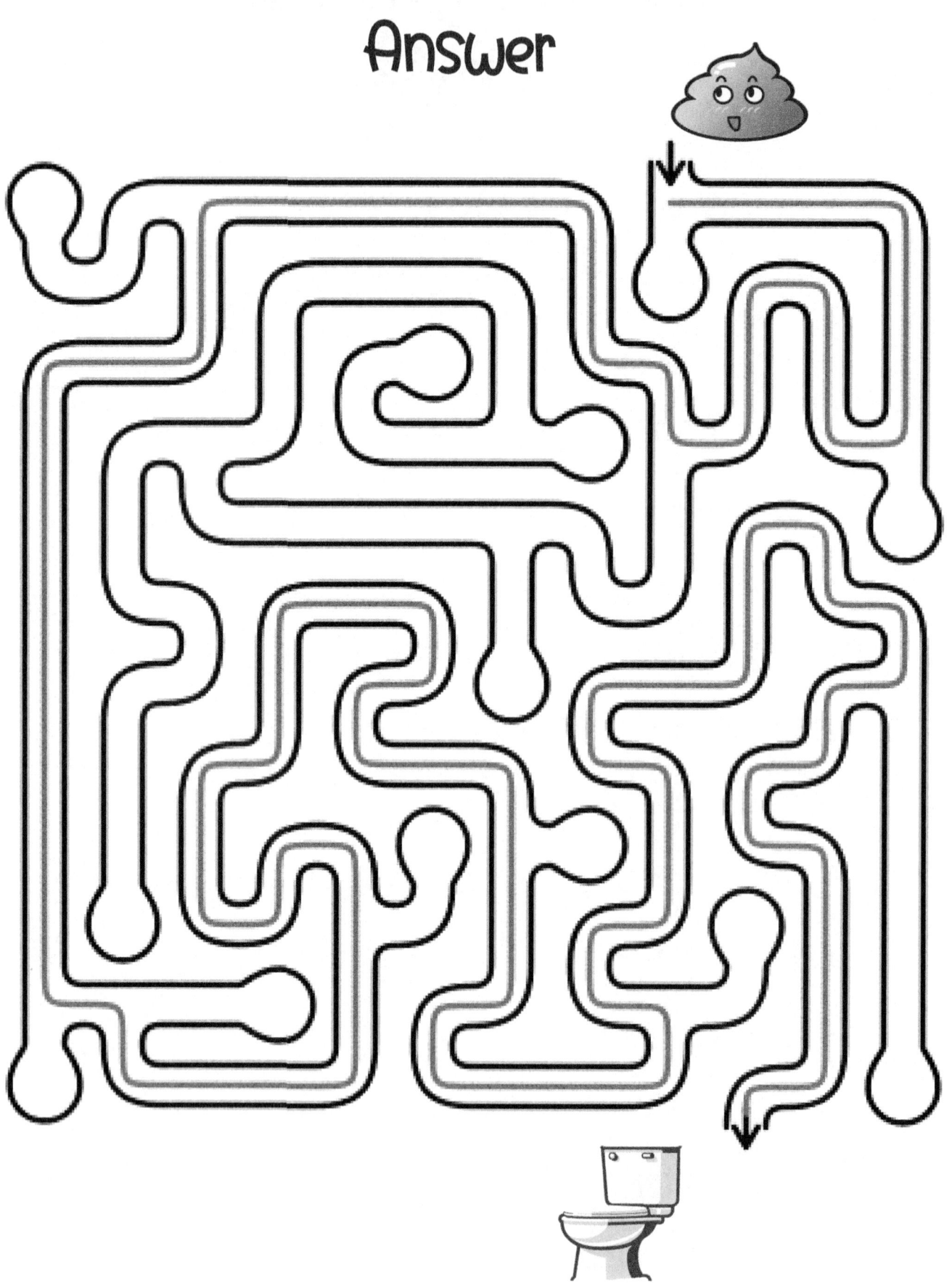

The Wizz Stinker Word Search Answers

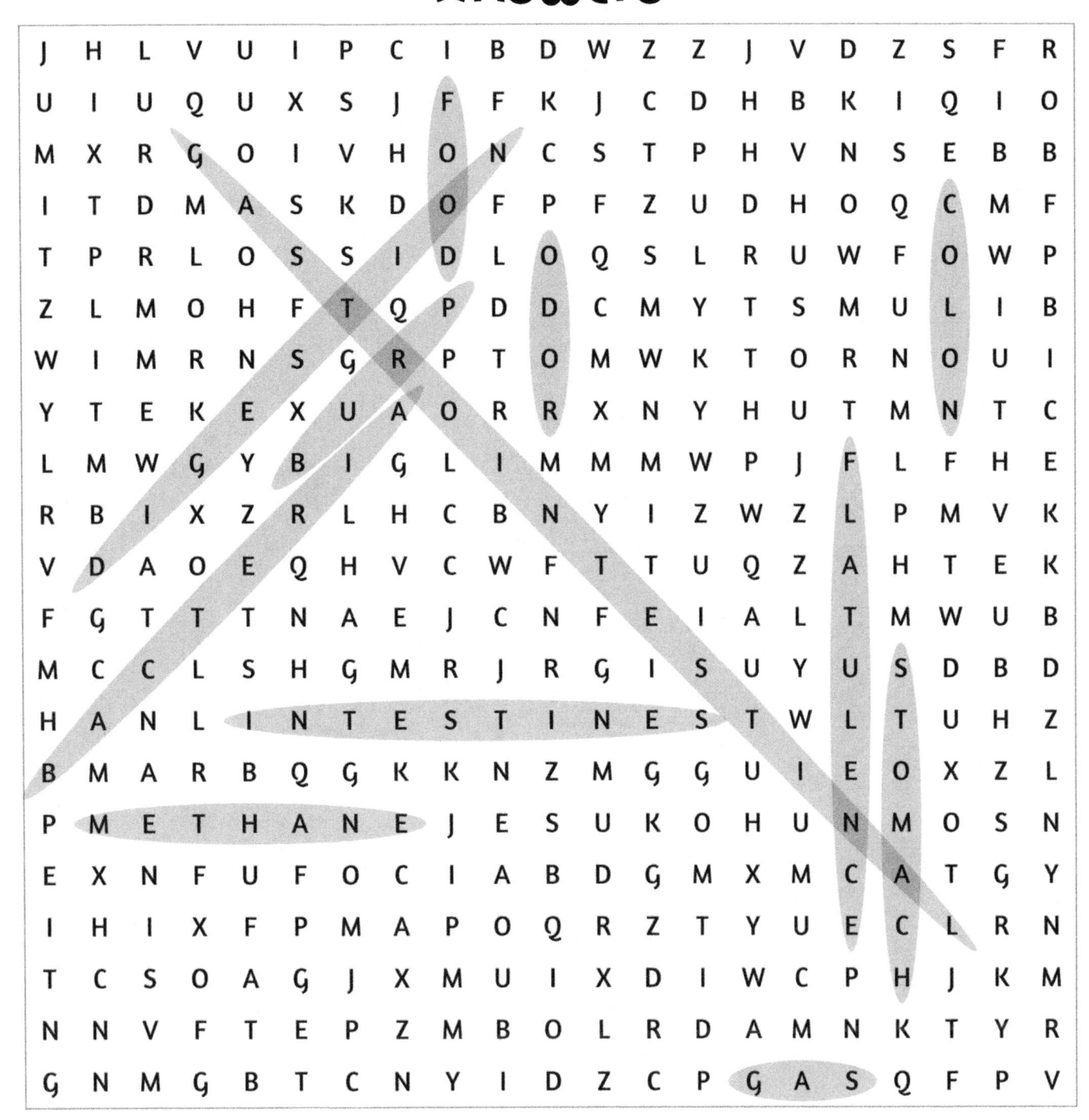

J	H	L	V	U	I	P	C	I	B	D	W	Z	Z	J	V	D	Z	S	F	R

(word search grid)

GAS
FOOD
STOMACH
FLATULENCE

ODOR
COLON
BACTERIA
INTESTINES

BURP
METHANE
DIGESTION
GASTROINTESTINAL

The Whiffy Science Word Puzzle Answers.

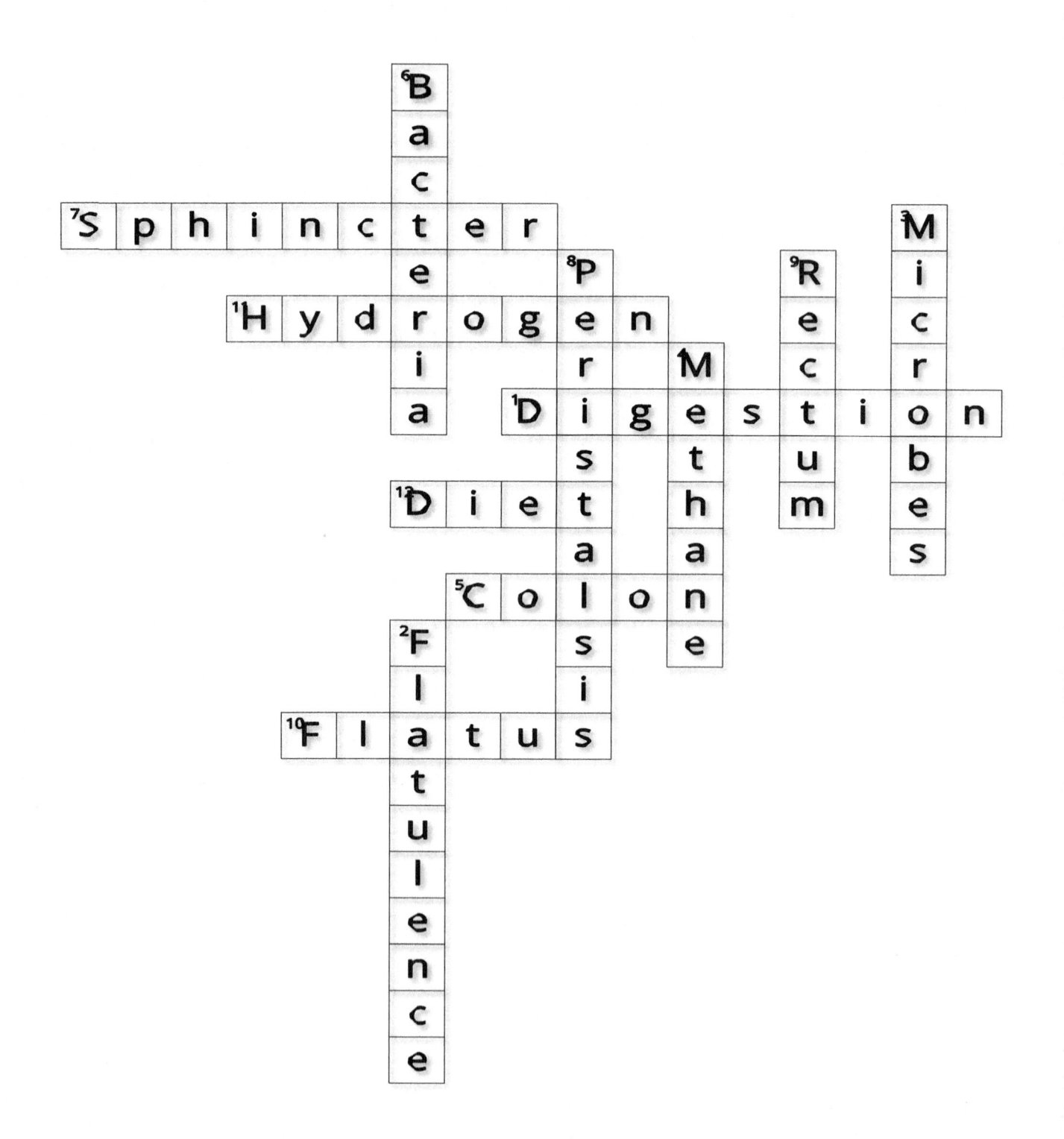

Across:
1. Hydrogen
4. Digestion
5. Colon
7. Sphincter
10. Flatus
12. Diet

Down:
2. Flatulence
3. Microbes
6. Bacteria
8. Peristalsis
9. Rectum
11. Methane

Windy Word Scramble Answers

sGa	GAS	eMnetha	METHANE
intsgiDeo	DIGESTION	etsnInesit	INTESTINES
aeaBticr	BACTERIA	olnCo	COLON
lautsF	FLATUS	Odro	ODOR
telonniratsiGats	GASTROINTESTINAL oelBw		BOWEL
emuRct	RECTUM	saesG	GASES
ntraiFemenot	FERMENTATION	ocMsrebi	MICROBES
tGu	GUT	iulgmbnR	RUMBLING
onrctexEi	EXCRETION	uoFl	FOUL
rgyHenod	HYDROGEN	uSlurf	SULFUR

The farting finale Quiz Answers

Part 1

1. 10-20

2. False (Not all animals fart; for example, birds and some species of sea life do not.)

3. Hydrogen sulfide

4. Cows

5. Flatulence

Part 2

1. D - Methane: While there are several gases that make up a fart (including nitrogen, hydrogen, and carbon dioxide), methane is often present in those who eat a lot of dietary fiber.

The farting finale Quiz Answers

2. B - Cows: Ruminant animals like cows produce large amounts of methane as part of their digestive process.

3. B - Due to sulfur-containing gases: Farts smell because of sulfur-containing gases that are produced by bacteria in your gut during digestion.

4. C - The vibration of the rectal opening: The sound comes from vibrations caused when gas exits your body quickly through a small opening—the same principle as letting air out of a balloon.

The farting finale Quiz Answers

5. A - Yes, it can cause discomfort and bloating: Holding in farts won't cause serious health problems, but it can lead to discomfort and bloating.

6. Answer: A and C - Some fish species use farting as a means of buoyancy control, and some communicate through a process similar to our tooting.

Amazing and well done to you. You have come to the end of your first Fabulously Funny Kids Book Of Farts where you have discovered the science, the facts, and the fun behind bottom burping and you have immersed yourself in some full-on interactive learning. You are now a fully-fledged farting genius.

I hope you have enjoyed this book and that it has made you laugh a lot. That reminds me, I know a poem all about laughing. It goes like this....

> One day I laughed and when I laughed, I farted!
> The more I farted the more I laughed and the more I laughed the more I farted.

Thank you.

If you have had fun do not forget to leave a review and let your friends and family know about the fun learning that you have had with this book.

Printed in Great Britain
by Amazon